Food in a Minute

3

Allyson Gofton

Hodder Moa Beckett

I would like to thank food assistant Sarah-Jane Gillies and photographers Alan Gillard and Nick Tresidder for the wonderful work they did on *Food in a Minute* – both the TV programme and the books.

The Wattie's products used in filming the programmes that make *Food in a Minute 3* were correct at the time of filming. However, from time to time names and can sizes alter, or products may be deleted. Please use a similar product if this should happen. – **Allyson Gofton.**

ISBN 1-86958-795–2

© 1999 – Original text, recipes and photographs by Allyson Gofton
The moral rights of the author have been asserted
© Food in a Minute, Mike O'Sullivan, Channel i, Allyson Gofton, Heinz Watties

© 1999 Design and format – Hodder Moa Beckett Publishers Limited

Published in 1999 by Hodder Moa Beckett Publishers Limited,
[a member of the Hodder Headline Group]
4 Whetu Place, Mairangi Bay, Auckland, New Zealand

Produced and designed by Hodder Moa Beckett Publishers Ltd
Photography by Alan Gillard and Nick Tresidder
Typesetting by Tradewinds

Film by Microdot, Auckland
Printed by McCollam's, Auckland

Contents

Introduction

It is 18 months since we produced our last *Food in a Minute* book. Time seems to have flown and cooking up new ideas for you has kept me and the *Food in a Minute* team very busy.

This, our third *Food in a Minute* book, marks over three and a half years or 175-plus programmes or meal ideas. The team is still together: Rob McLaughlin, our director, has continued to find new ways for me to present my 'intros' and 'outros' and creatively film each recipe.

Cameraman Rhys Duncan took a six month break to film a movie in Wellington and we were joined by Alistair Crombie. It was déjà-vu for Al and me as we had worked together filming a Graham Kerr series some 10 years earlier, when he was cameraman and I was Graham's food assistant.

Sarah-Jane Gillies, my right hand lady, returned after daughter Poppy-May turned one. I would be lost without her effervescent personality that brings sunshine to every day we work together. Jo Bain has continued to be our on-set production manager for three years and during winter this year took over the director's reins while Rob and Michelle were on holiday in London.

On sound, Bernie Wright still never misses a beat and he has kept his cans or earphones firmly on, listening for the perfect sizzle or can-opening noise for 175 programmes!

And if that sounds tough, Sue Arts on make-up and hair styling has continued to search town for new outfits for me to wear each programme that will suit the style of dish, and keep me looking good.

The *Food In A Minute* **team.**

(left to right): Louise Moore, set assistant; Rhys Duncan, cameraman; Rob McLaughlin, director; Bernie Wright, sound; Moi; Jo Bain, producer; Sarah-Jane Gillies, food assistant; Sue Arts, make up artist; Adrian Greshoff, lighting.

With our constantly evolving set, Ado Greshoff, gaffer, has worked hard to keep the lighting looking great; he's a real perfectionist, wanting the kitchen, food and me to always look our best.

At Heinz Wattie we have seen many changes. Vivienne Kerr, our trusted *Food in a Minute* manager, has been transferred to London and looking after us now is Di Handley, fellow food writer and home economist for Heinz Wattie, while John Macdonald, business manager for Heinz Wattie, has remained our most faithful supporter, always there to deal with any major concerns.

There are new faces at the desks of the product managers, all keen to see that whatever we cook with their product is going to be a winner. Heinz Wattie has continued to be a look-ahead company, developing new products that encourage people to keep cooking, while removing much of the stress and hassle from meal preparation.

Mike O'Sullivan, executive producer, has had an

Plucking saffron.

exciting year building a new home and launching many new projects at his company, Channel i, while Colin Follas, joint executive producer, whose company Tiger Films produces the series, has kept us all under control.

The hard work of each of these people has resulted in *Food in a Minute* winning awards in 1998 for its outstanding marketing success. The New Zealand Guild of Food Writers awarded *Food in a Minute* with

The Wattie's team.

Viv Kerr, left; Di Handley, 3rd from left; John Macdonald, last right; and their colleagues.

(left) Stalls at the Marrakech night market; (right) Traditional Moroccan breakfast.

Food Writer of the Year (advertising category). We also won the coveted 1998 TVNZ/Marketing Magazine awards for marketing in the very competitive Fast Moving Consumer Goods category.

On a lighter side, Warwick and I have had the opportunity to pack our haversacks and travel with Alan Gillard, photographer, a couple of times. Last year we sought out the mysterious saffron spice in the parched plains of La Mancha, Spain. Saffron flowers for only 10 days a year and we went to participate in the harvest and experience the country festival at

Consuegra that celebrates the saffron harvest every year. We detoured to Morocco - a magical country where it was like stepping back in time - to seek out the most flavoursome tagines, or Moroccan casseroles, in cities like Marrakech, Fez and Meknes, where their traditional way of life seems to have hardly changed.

Graham's Port located in the Douro River.

We finished with a spectacular train ride up the Duoro Valley in Portugal to see the home and manufacture of Graham's port. In O'Porto, you could have been forgiven for thinking you had travelled back to the time of Dickens. Majestic old buildings that had seen better times hid the crumbling World Heritage Riberia district that flanks the Duoro River.

This year it was the vanilla pod that Warwick, Alan and I wanted to find out more about. Grown in the humid, mountainous terrain of Moorea, Tahiti, the vanilla orchid flowers for only one day each year

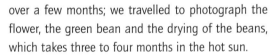

Vanilla beans before and after drying.

Gisborne, Christchurch, Kaikoura, Whakatane, Rotorua, Timaru, and Oamaru, raising money for local charities. Each visit was special and it has been a pleasure to help where I can to raise funds for schools, Parent and Child Centres, Rotary, Zonta Clubs and others.

The recipes in *Food in a Minute 3* are a compilation of my favourites from the last 18 months and I hope you will find them and the cooking tips and hints in this book as useful as the first two.

Cheers

over a few months; we travelled to photograph the flower, the green bean and the drying of the beans, which takes three to four months in the hot sun.

If the flowers are not pollinated before the midday sun, they will not bear fruit! No wonder pure vanilla is so expensive.

To travel and experience all this has been incredibly rewarding and exciting, giving me the opportunity to write about the spices and flavourings that we take so much for granted and that add colour and flavour to our culinary world.

The video footage from each trip has also added interest to my presentations when I travel around New Zealand on fund-raising demonstrations.

This year we have visited Tutukaka, Whangarei, Tauranga, Havelock North, Hamilton, Waipukurau,

light
meals

Many ideas I present do not quite fit the Main Meals chapter: wonderful suggestions for salads, soups, tacos, mini pizzas, soufflés and fritters. Easy ideas perfect for brunching, snacking or a light meal are here to tempt you.

Pumpkin Soup *with* Thai Topping

Pumpkin marries well with spicy foods and this quick topping turns a family favourite soup into something special.

Preparation Time 10-15 minutes

Cooking Time 5 minutes

Serves 4

INGREDIENTS

- ¼ cup desiccated or thread coconut
- ½ cup peanuts
- 1 tblsp minced fresh ginger
- 2 tblsp chopped fresh mint
- 2 tblsp chopped fresh chives
- 2 x 600 gram pouches **Wattie's Harvest Pumpkin Soup**
- about ¼ cup coconut cream

METHOD

1. Toast the coconut in a 180°C oven for about 2-3 minutes until the coconut is lightly coloured. Roast the peanuts at 180°C for 10 minutes until golden. Cool and then rub between your hands to remove the skins. Chop the peanuts finely. (Or use roasted, unsalted peanuts.)

2. In a bowl mix together the toasted coconut, peanuts, ginger, mint and chives.

3. Heat the soup and pour into four bowls. Spoon on top a little coconut cream and sprinkle over the toasted coconut crumble.

Cook's Tip

When we were in Morocco we enjoyed mint tea daily. A glass cup was packed full of mint and freshly brewed tea was poured over. The mint leaves were left in if you had tea without sugar. Try this at home – it is especially refreshing in summer.

Country Tomato *and* Vegetable Soup
with Parsley Pesto Croutons

Pestos have become extremely popular and now we can purchase anything from the traditional basil pesto to sundried tomato or pepper. Pestos are also easy and economical to make.

Try variations like this one.

Cook's Tip

Freeze the pesto in ice cubes. Once frozen, transfer the pesto cubes to a freezer bag and freeze. Add a cube to your favourite pasta sauce, winter soup or even to a summer salad dressing.

INGREDIENTS

- ½ small French breadstick
- 1 cup firmly packed parsley leaves and stalks
- 1 clove garlic, crushed and peeled
- ½ cup toasted cashew nuts
- 1 cup grated cheddar cheese (or use ½ grated cheddar and ½ grated parmesan)
- ¼ cup oil (olive or canola is best)
- salt and pepper
- 2 x 600 gram pouches **Wattie's Dining In Country Tomato and Vegetable Soup**

METHOD

1. To make the croutons, slice the French breadstick into 0.5 cm slices and grill on one side only.

2. In a food processor put the parsley, garlic, cashew nuts and half the cheese and process until finely chopped.

3. Gradually pour the oil down the feed tube while the machine is running to make a smooth paste. Season with salt and pepper.

4. Heat the soup and pour into 4 bowls.

5. Spread a teaspoon of the pesto on top of each crouton and place in the soup. Sprinkle each bowl with the remaining grated cheese. Place bowls on a baking tray and grill under a high heat until the cheese is melted. Transfer to a serving plate to serve.

Preparation Time 15 minutes

Cooking Time 10 minutes

Serves 4

Chuckwagon Hash Fritters

Fritters are a weekend breakfast or light meal favourite. This recipe proved popular as it makes use of Hashbrowns in place of mashed potato. A light hand is needed when mixing the ingredients together, to ensure the fritters are light in texture when cooked.

INGREDIENTS

▶ 360 gram bag **Wattie's Frozen Hashbrowns**

▶ 1 cup **Wattie's Frozen Chuckwagon Corn**

▶ 4 spring onions, trimmed and finely chopped

▶ ½ cup self-raising flour

▶ ½ tsp salt

▶ 2 eggs

▶ 1 cup milk

▶ ¼ cup chopped parsley

▶ 1 tblsp mustard (optional)

METHOD

1 Defrost the Hashbrowns for 1 minute in the microwave, then chop into 1 cm dice.

2 In a bowl toss together the diced Hashbrowns, corn, spring onions, self-raising flour and salt.

3 In a clean bowl or jug beat together the eggs, milk, parsley and mustard. Gently stir the milk into the Hashbrown mix.

4 Cook large spoonfuls in a hot, greased frying pan for about 4 minutes on each side, turning once only. Serve hot with grilled bacon and golden syrup.

Preparation Time 10-15 minutes

Cooking Time 8-10 minutes

Makes 12

Cook's Tip

When eating out or reading US recipe books you often see mentioned 'maple syrup', 'corn syrup' and 'golden syrup'. Here's a quick rundown on each.

• **Golden Syrup** is a by-product from refining sugarcane. The syrup that remains after crystallised sugar is extracted from the concentrated cane juice is refined to produce golden syrup or treacle. It will last for ages, and I prefer it best when using it in Golden Syrup Dumplings.

• **Maple Syrup** is the syrup tapped from the maple tree. Once collected, the syrup is boiled until much of the water has evaporated and the sap is thick and syrupy. It takes between 90 and 225 litres to produce 4½ litres of syrup, depending on how thick the sap is when it is tapped. As producing it is a labour-intensive process, true maple syrup is expensive, but delicious. Often we see mentioned maple-flavoured syrup, which is corn syrup flavoured with maple syrup. Pure maple syrup can be interchanged with golden syrup.

• **Corn Syrup** is a thick syrup created by mixing corn starch with acids or enzymes. The resulting thick syrup is clarified and bottled. As it inhibits crystallisation, corn syrup is often included in icings and confectionery. It is tasteless and is available in the sugar section of the supermarket.

Mexican *Ranch-style* Eggs

In Mexico these are called Huevos Rancheros or Ranch–style eggs. They're ideal for brunch or lunch. Serve them with extra tortillas, toast or bread and a crispy salad.

Cook's Tip

If you like chilli, add a chopped fresh red chilli pepper or dried red chilli with the tomatoes. Be careful when deseeding fresh chilli: the material that burns you, called capsicain, is mainly located in the membrane surrounding the seeds. Use gloves and/or wash your hands thoroughly afterwards, cleaning especially under your nails.

INGREDIENTS

- 4 rashers rindless bacon, finely chopped
- 1 onion, peeled and finely chopped
- 2 tblsp oil
- 400 gram can **Wattie's Mexican Spiced Tomatoes**
- 2 tblsp finely chopped coriander or parsley
- 4 eggs

METHOD

1. Cook the bacon and onion in the oil in a frying pan over a moderate heat for about 5-7 minutes until the bacon and onion are golden and very fragrant.

2. Add the spiced tomatoes and coriander or parsley and simmer for 2 minutes.

3. Make 4 wells in the centre of the sauce and break an egg into each well.

4. Cover and simmer for about 4 minutes until the eggs are cooked.

   Serve each egg with a little sauce on top of a warm tortilla or a slice of buttered toast.

Preparation Time 10 minutes

Cooking Time 15 minutes

Serves 4

Ham *and* Courgette Pasta

This dish is perfect in summer, when courgettes are at their cheapest. Try smoked chicken in place of ham for a change.

Cook's Tip

Spread pizza bases with garlic butter and grill until hot and golden to make this tasty garlic bread.

INGREDIENTS

- 4 cups large shell pasta (large or small)
- boiling salted water
- dash of oil to pan-fry
- 4 large courgettes, trimmed and grated
- 5-6 spring onions, trimmed and finely chopped
- 2-3 ham steaks, diced
- 400 gram can **Wattie's Creamy Herb and Garlic Stir-in Pasta Sauce**
- ½ cup milk or chicken stock

METHOD

1. Cook the pasta in the boiling salted water for 12-15 minutes until al dente (firm to the bite). Drain well and keep warm.

2. Heat the oil in a frying pan, add the courgettes and spring onion and cook over a moderately high heat for about 5 minutes, stirring regularly.

3. Add the ham, pasta sauce and milk or stock. Simmer for 3-4 minutes until hot.

4. Toss the well-drained pasta through the sauce and serve with garlic bread to the side.

Preparation Time 15 minutes
Cooking Time 15 minutes
Serves 4

Tropical Summer Salad

This rice salad was a great hit with the crew, who thoroughly enjoyed its tropical flavours.

Cook's Tip

Fresh mangoes are wonderful and sometimes in winter we get them very cheaply, imported from South America. They're a real treat during the cooler months. Here's an easy way to remove the flesh from the fruit:

1. Cut down lengthwise on either side of the large, flat stone that sits in the middle of the mango.
2. Take the mango slice and place it skin side down in your hand. With a sharp paring knife, cut through the flesh to the skin (but without going through the skin) on a diagonal.
3. Then cut on the opposite angle to make a diamond pattern.
4. Push the mango upwards from underneath so the flesh stands proud and scoop out the diamond-shaped fruit. Once you have mastered this, you'll be able to do it in no time. And as for the flesh on the stone – it's best sucked off by children who will love it.

INGREDIENTS

- 2 litres or 8 cups water
- 2 tsp salt
- 1½ cups long-grain rice
- ½ **Tegel Smoked Chicken**
- 400 gram can **Wattie's Baby Corn**, well drained
- 1 cup chopped tropical fruit, such as pawpaw, mangoes or pineapple
- 5-6 spring onions, trimmed and chopped
- 3 cm piece fresh ginger, grated

Dressing
- 1 cup **Wattie's Mayonnaise**
- ½ cup coconut milk
- grated rind and juice of two large oranges

METHOD

1. Bring the water and salt to the boil. Sprinkle in the rice slowly and boil rapidly for 12 minutes. Drain through a colander and rinse with plenty of cold water to arrest the cooking. Drain well.

2. Pull the meat from the chicken bones and shred finely.

3. In a large bowl toss together the cooled rice, smoked chicken, corn, tropical fruit, spring onion and grated ginger.

4. For the dressing mix together the mayonnaise, coconut milk, orange rind and juice and toss through.

Preparation Time 25-30 minutes

Serves 6-8

Mini Pizza *Nibbles*

INGREDIENTS

- 2 sheets pre-rolled puff pastry, defrosted
- 300 ml can **Wattie's Pizza Topping**
- 1 cup grated cheese (parmesan, cheddar or edam)
- chopped black or stuffed green olives and parsley to decorate

METHOD

1. Cut 6 cm circles from each of the pastry sheets and place on a greased baking tray.

2. Place a heaped teaspoonful of the pizza topping in the centre of each round and sprinkle over a little grated cheese.

3. Bake at 220°C for 10 minutes until the pastry is well risen and golden and the filling is hot. Sprinkle each with chopped olives and parsley before serving.

   Note: If you do not have any puff pastry, you can use **Wattie's Pizza Topping** on crostini made from French breadsticks and garnished with a slice of feta, brie or camembert cheese. To make crostini, slice a French stick into 0.5 cm rounds and bake at the top of a 180°C oven for 10 minutes, turning once.

Preparation Time 10 minutes

Cooking Time 10 minutes

Makes 20

This is a very easy nibble idea on which you can make many variations, such as those below.

Topping Variations

- Use grated mozzarella and blue cheese with glazed onions or onion marmalade.

- Use olive tapenade and feta cheese.

- Use basil pesto and bocconcini or cheddar cheese.

- Use cream cheese, smoked salmon, avocado slices and a little grated mozzarella.

Cook's Tip

Crostini can be made in advance and stored in an airtight container. Here crostini have been prepared from French bread and ciabatta.

INGREDIENTS

- 12 slices streaky bacon, rind removed
- 400 gram packet **Wattie's Frozen Potato Medallions**
- 2 eggs
- 125 grams cream cheese
- ½ cup cream
- 2 tblsp chopped dill or parsley
- 340 gram can **Wattie's Asparagus Spears**, well drained

METHOD

1. Stretch the bacon rashers with the back of a large cook's knife and use them to line the base of a 25 cm x 11 cm x 7 cm loaf tin (see photo).

2. Defrost the potato medallions in the microwave for 2 minutes, then cut into 1-2 cm chunks.

3. In a bowl blend together the eggs, cream cheese, cream and dill or parsley. Fold in the chopped medallions.

4. Place one third of the mixture in the loaf tin. Arrange half the asparagus spears on top and repeat these layers, ending with the potato mix. Fold over any bacon ends.

5. Bake at 200°C for 40 minutes.

   Allow to stand for 10 minutes before turning out of the tin and slicing.

Preparation Time 30 minutes

Cooking Time 40 minutes

Standing Time 10 minutes

Serves 4-6

Asparagus Slice

This rather decadent savoury slice was a great hit. It looks great and is best eaten warm with a crisp green salad.

Cook's Tip

Open your asparagus can upside down to protect the delicate spears.

It is a good idea, when you're using bacon rashers to wrap around the outside of a loaf or a piece of meat, to stretch them with the back of a heavy knife. Streaky bacon will stretch quite significantly, making it easier to handle and producing a better-looking dish.

INGREDIENTS

- 1 medium-sized aubergine
- 1 tblsp salt
- 1 red pepper
- 1 yellow pepper
- 2 courgettes, trimmed
- oil for basting
- 250 grams green or yellow beans, stringed
- 1 punnet baby tomatoes, washed
- 6 flat mushrooms (or 10 baby mushrooms)

Dressing
- ½ cup **ETA Gourmet Garlic or Gourmet Red Pepper Dressing**
- 2 tblsp each chopped chives and parsley

METHOD

1. Cut the aubergine into 0.5 cm slices. Sprinkle the slices with salt, layer them in a colander and set aside for 30 minutes. (This allows the bitter juices to run free.) Rinse well under cold water and pat dry on absorbent paper.

2. Cut the red and yellow peppers into quarters, discarding the core and seeds. Cut the courgettes lengthways into thick slices.

3. Heat the barbecue until hot. Brush all the vegetables with oil, place them on the barbecue and cook quickly over a high heat. The vegetables will blacken, but in doing so become quite sweet.

4. Arrange the vegetables on a platter and pour on the dressing. Serve warm.

Dressing

Combine all ingredients.

Grilled *Summer* Salad

Serving vegetables roasted or grilled, dressed with vinaigrette, is popular, easy and delicious. With this salad, the vegetables can cook on the barbecue at the same time as the meat or chicken. Season well with salt and pepper for good flavour.

Preparation Time 30 minutes

Cooking Time 10 minutes

Serves 4

INGREDIENTS

- ¾ cup hummus (recipe follows)
- 2 large pizza bases (from the supermarket)
- 300 gram bottle **Wattie's Bit on the Side Oriental Plum Sauce**
- 100 grams crumbled feta
- 1 cup grated cheddar cheese
- 200 grams shaved ham or 1 double breast smoked chicken, finely shredded
- 1 courgette, trimmed and very thinly sliced
- 1 red pepper, cored, seeded and very thinly sliced

METHOD

1. Spread the hummus evenly over the two pizza bases. Sprinkle liberally with plum sauce.

2. Sprinkle over the feta and half the grated cheese.

3. Top with the ham or chicken, courgette and peppers.

4. Sprinkle over the remaining grated cheese and a little more plum sauce if wished.

5. Bake at 230°C at the top of the oven for 15 minutes until the pizza is piping hot. Serve immediately.

Preparation Time 10 minutes

Cooking Time 15 minutes

Serves 6

Oriental Plum
Pizza
with
Hummus

Wood-fired oven pizzas with all manner of toppings are so popular that we decided to do this hummus and ham plum sauce version. It tastes fabulous and is a very healthy dish.

Pizza Variations

Using the **Wattie's Bit on the Side** range, you can create an almost endless variety of pizzas. Try one of these:

- Hummus, finely sliced lamb, Gourmet BBQ Sauce, red peppers, feta and olives.
- Basil pesto, crème fraiche or sour cream, a few sliced scallops, mozzarella, shredded courgettes, yellow peppers and Sweet Chilli Sauce.
- Java Satay Sauce, shredded smoked chicken, bok choy, peanuts, sprinkling curry powder and feta.
- Hummus, Spicy Tomato Sauce, sliced rare beef, broccoli florets, mozzarella cheese and an olive or two.

Hummus

INGREDIENTS

- 300 gram can **Craig's Chickpeas in Brine**, well drained
- 2 cloves garlic, crushed, peeled and chopped
- ½ tsp each salt
- ½ tsp cayenne pepper
- 2 tblsp oil
- juice 1 lemon

METHOD

1. Put everything in the food processor and process until smooth.

   Note: You can also buy hummus in the delicatessen or chiller section of your supermarket.

Preparation Time 5 minutes

Makes 1 cup

Made-In-One-Pan
Dinner

This dish is great for flatters and teenagers to make, and as it is all cooked in one pan there are hardly any dishes to wash. As an alternative, when cooked, place the mixture in a pie dish, top with Wattie's Potato Pom Poms, a little grated cheese and bake until golden and hot.

Cook's Tip

To keep herbs fresh, rinse them under water and shake off any excess. Place them in a plastic bag; blow it up with your own breath, then seal the bag tightly and store it in the refrigerator. Freshen the herbs every 2 or 3 days. You'll find they will keep well like this for many days.

Preparation Time 15 minutes

Cooking Time 30-35 minutes

Serves 4

INGREDIENTS

- 1 onion, peeled and diced
- 500 grams **Quality Mark Lean Minced Beef**
- 2 tblsp oil
- 1 large golden kumara, peeled and diced
- 2 tsp Marmite, Vegemite or Promite
- 1 tblsp flour
- ½ cup **Wattie's Tomato Sauce**
- 1½ cups water
- ½ x 750 gram bag **Wattie's Chuckwagon Corn**
- salt and pepper to season

METHOD

1 Cook the onion and mince in the oil in a large, lidded frying pan over a high heat for 4-5 minutes, until the onion has softened and the mince has browned. Break up the mince with the back of a wooden spoon or a fork as you go. It is best to do this in two batches, otherwise the mince will stew rather than brown. Stir in the kumara.

2 In a jug mix together the Marmite, flour, tomato sauce and water and pour over the mince. Cover and simmer gently for 10-15 minutes until the kumara is almost cooked.

3 Add the corn mix and stir. Cover and simmer for a further 10 minutes. Season with salt and pepper if wished.

Pizza Pie

A simple variation of one of our favourite takeaways. Add freshly chopped herbs like basil, rosemary or parsley to the filling, or even anchovies, if you're a fan.

Cook's Tip

Handle a scone dough as delicately and quickly as you can, to ensure lightness.

This is what my *Food in a Minute* set looks like when we're filming from afar and from behind Rhys Duncan's camera. The crew go to enormous lengths to get the very best shots they can, which they hope will encourage you to cook each dish I prepare.

INGREDIENTS

- 250 gram piece mild salami, finely diced
- 425 gram can **Wattie's Tomato and Onion Pasta Sauce**
- ¼ cup finely chopped stuffed olives
- 1 red pepper, deseeded and finely chopped (optional)
- 3 cups self-raising flour
- 50 grams butter
- 1½ cups grated cheddar cheese
- 1½ cups milk

METHOD

1. Mix the salami, pasta sauce, olives and pepper together.

2. Sift the flour into a bowl and rub or cut in the butter. Stir in 1 cup of the cheese and make a well in the centre. Pour in the milk and mix to form a soft dough.

3. Turn out onto a floured board and knead lightly. Roll out to a 35-40 cm round and drape evenly over a 23 cm loose-bottom flan tin.

4. Spoon the salami filling inside. Flip over the edges (they will not completely touch) and sprinkle the remaining cheese on top.

5. Fan bake in the middle of the oven at 200°C (or bake at 220°C) for 30-35 minutes until the pie is well risen, hot and golden. Serve warm.

Preparation Time 30 minutes

Cooking Time 35 minutes

Serves 4

Cheat's Soufflé

INGREDIENTS

- about 25 grams butter
- 10 slices white bread
- 4 rashers bacon, chopped and cooked until crisp
- 4 eggs
- 415 gram can **Wattie's Cream Style Corn**
- 2 cups milk
- ½ cup grated cheddar cheese

METHOD

1. Butter the bread slices and sandwich together to make 5 sandwiches. Trim the crusts from each and cut into quarters.

2. Arrange the bread randomly in a 2-litre ovenproof dish. Sprinkle over the bacon.

3. In a large bowl or jug blend together the eggs, corn and milk. Pour over the bread evenly and then sprinkle over the cheese.

4. Fan bake at 180°C (or 200°C bake) for 30 minutes. Serve hot.

Preparation Time 15 minutes

Cooking Time 30 minutes

Serves 4-6

This quick and simple soufflé is ideal for an easy family lunch or light meal. For a change use a can of Wattie's Asparagus pieces.

Recommendation

I prefer to use 'Look' cookware for *Food in a Minute* and at home. Its steel reinforced coating ensures even heat distribution and being non-stick you can cut down on the amount of oil or butter used for pan-frying and have no fears of food like milk pudding sticking to the saucepan sides. When buying saucepans, choose the sizes that best suit your requirements. I have medium and large sizes as I rarely need a small saucepan. A large stock pot, casserole size, doubles as a pasta pot and casserole and the handles can be safely placed in the oven. Buy good-quality saucepans to begin with and they will last for ages.

Boston Baked Beans

There are many versions of this dish. Using **Wattie's Baked Beans** cuts out much preparation time. Add extra zest with a good pouring of dark rum just before serving!

- 4 pork slices, rind removed
- dash of oil
- 2 onions, peeled and finely chopped
- 1 tsp minced garlic
- 1 tblsp dry mustard
- 2 tblsp brown sugar
- ¼ cup golden syrup
- 2 x 425 gram cans **Wattie's Baked Beans**
- ¼ cup **Lea and Perrins Worcestershire Sauce**
- ¼ cup **Wattie's Homestyle Tomato Sauce**

1. Cut the pork into 1 cm wide pieces. Heat the oil in a large, heat-proof casserole and cook the pork over a moderate heat until well browned.

2. Add the onion and garlic and cook for a further 2 minutes.

3. Add the mustard, brown sugar, golden syrup, baked beans, Worcestershire sauce and tomato sauce.

4. Stir, cover and simmer gently for about 10 minutes. Serve hot with toast for brunch or with green vegetables for dinner.

Sarah-Jane and I spend time each week answering the many readers' queries that I receive. On one occasion a viewer kindly sent me a copy of a very old manual: I was delighted, as reading old cookbooks and manuals is like reviewing the history of our cuisine.

Preparation Time 10 minutes

Cooking Time 20 minutes

Serves 4

main
meals

Feel like something new and different tonight for dinner? In this chapter there's a fabulous selection to tempt you with. Stir-fries, risotto, casseroles and roasts: they're all here with plenty of tips and information to make the time you spend cooking in the kitchen easier and more enjoyable.

Lamb Shanks in Red Wine

with Country Nugget Potatoes

When this recipe featured on TV, John Macdonald at Heinz Wattie received a phone call from a viewer suggesting Heinz Wattie might like to market six-legged sheep as the country sold out of lamb shanks in one week! This is a great winter dish.

INGREDIENTS

- 6-8 **Quality Mark Lamb Shanks**
- dash of oil
- 10-12 baby onions, peeled and left whole
- 4 rashers bacon, diced
- 10-12 button mushrooms, wiped
- 1 cup red wine
- 550 gram can **Wattie's Just Add Hearty Mince Simmer Sauce**
- 750 gram packet **Wattie's Frozen Golden Nugget Potatoes**
- 2 sprigs rosemary
- 4-6 cloves garlic, crushed but not peeled

METHOD

1 Brown the lamb shanks in the dash of oil in a flame-proof casserole.

2 Add the onion, bacon, mushrooms, red wine and simmer sauce and bring to the boil. Cover and cook in the oven at 180°C for 1½ hours until tender.

Nuggets

3 Arrange the potato nuggets in a baking dish with the rosemary and garlic and bake at 220°C for 20 minutes, shaking occasionally.

Serve the lamb and nuggets garnished with a little fresh chopped rosemary if wished.

Preparation Time 15 minutes

Cooking Time 1½ hours

Serves 4

Cook's Tip

'Flame-proof' means a casserole that is able to withstand direct heat on top of a stove. These are usually cast-iron, or non-stick such as Look Cookware casseroles. If you do not have a flame-proof casserole, brown your meat, onions, etc, in a frying pan and transfer to a casserole to cook.

INGREDIENTS

- 8 **Tegel Chicken Drumsticks**
- dash of oil
- 2 onions, peeled and finely chopped
- 1 cup finely sliced dried apricots
- 1 tsp ground ginger
- 1 tsp ground coriander
- 1 cup chicken stock
- 400 gram can **Wattie's Mediterranean Tomatoes**

To Garnish
- a few black olives (optional)
- chopped parsley or coriander

METHOD

1. Remove the skin from the drumsticks.

2. Brown the chicken in the oil over a moderate heat in a large, lidded frying pan until golden on all sides.

3. Add the onions, apricots, ginger, coriander, stock and tomatoes and bring to the boil.

4. Cover and simmer gently for 30 minutes, until the chicken drumsticks are cooked.

   Serve garnished if wished with black olives, chopped parsley or coriander.

   Preparation Time 15 minutes

   Cooking Time 40 minutes

   Serves 4

Moroccan *Chicken and* Apricot Stew

Rather than serve this really delicious stew on rice, try couscous for a change. It only takes 5 minutes to cook.

Cook's Tip

New Zealand dried apricots have far more flavour than the imported varieties, although they may not look as plump.

To cook couscous, place equal quantities of instant couscous and boiling water or stock in a bowl and stand for 5 minutes until the couscous has absorbed all the moisture. Fluff up with a fork and season well with salt and pepper. You can flavour the couscous with a knob of butter or a dash of oil (olive is nice), as well as with spices, herbs, nuts and fruit, or with pastes such as pesto: it is up to you.

Butter Chicken
Under a Sesame Seed Pastry Crust

Filo pastry is fun to work with. We scrunched it up into bundles to place on top of this pie and the end result looks spectacular. Use it for your favourite pie – sweet or savoury.

Cook's Tip

If you do not have any filo, cover the pie with a 400 gram packet of puff pastry, glaze with milk and sprinkle with the sesame seeds before baking.

Preparation Time 15 minutes

Cooking Time 45 minutes

Serves 4

INGREDIENTS

▶ 500 grams pumpkin, peeled and diced into 1 cm pieces
▶ 1 onion, peeled and finely chopped
▶ dash of oil
▶ 8 boneless **Tegel Chicken Thighs**, skin removed
▶ ½ cup dried sultanas
▶ 415 gram can **Wattie's Butter Chicken Curry Sauce**
▶ 12-16 sheets filo pastry
▶ 100 grams butter, melted
▶ 3 tblsp sesame seeds

METHOD

1 Cook the pumpkin and onion in the oil in a large, lidded frying pan over a moderate heat for about 10 minutes until the pumpkin is browned and partially cooked. Set aside.

2 Cut the chicken pieces into thirds, add to the frying pan and brown over a higher heat. Return the pumpkin and onion to the pan with the sultanas and curry sauce. Cover and simmer gently for 15 minutes.

3 Transfer to a 6-cup-capacity pie dish.

4 Take 1 sheet of filo pastry, brush with butter and sprinkle lightly with sesame seeds. Place another sheet on top and repeat until you have 4 sheets of filo. Place these on top of the pie dish and turn the edges of the filo over to fit.

5 Brush the remaining sheets with butter and scrunch up and place on top of the filo-covered pie. Sprinkle over the sesame seeds.

6 Bake at 190°C for 20 minutes. Serve hot.

Hunter-style Chicken

The chicken for this recipe is tossed in seasoned flour before pan–frying, to add colour and help thicken the sauce. Add a touch of ground paprika or chilli for extra flavour.

Cook's Tip

Rice is a great product to keep on hand at all times. Long-grain rice varieties include:

JASMINE RICE – great for Thai and Asian meals;

BASMATI RICE – expensive and intensely fragrant, it can be used for special Indian dinners;

PLAIN LONG-GRAIN RICE – ideal for wherever you want light, fluffy and separate rice grains.

Short-grain rice varieties include:

ABORIO RICE – very starchy and used mainly for Italian risottos;

CALROSE RICE – an Australian medium/short-grain;

SUSHI RICE – sticky, starchy rice that is ideal for sushi making.

Short-grain rices are best used when you want a close-textured product like rice pudding, risotto or a paella. Both long and short-grain rices are available as white or brown and each has variable cooking times, depending on the rice variety. Always check the instructions on the back of the packet. Wild rice is not really rice, but the seed of a grass grown mainly in America, and now in Australia. It takes up to 50 minutes to cook.

Preparation Time 15 minutes

Cooking Time 40 minutes

Serves 4

INGREDIENTS

- 8 Tegel Chicken Drumsticks
- ¼ cup seasoned flour
- 2-3 tblsp oil
- 2 onions, peeled and sliced
- 250 grams mushrooms, quartered
- 425 gram can **Wattie's Garlic Pasta Sauce**
- 2 tblsp chopped fresh rosemary
- 2 big garlic cloves, crushed, peeled and sliced (optional)

Rice
- 2 tblsp oil
- 1 onion, peeled and finely chopped
- 2 cups long-grain rice
- 3 cups hot water or chicken stock
- 1 tsp salt

METHOD

1. Remove the skin from the chicken.
2. Toss the chicken in the seasoned flour.
3. Heat the oil in a lidded frying pan, add the chicken and brown well.
4. Add the onion, mushrooms, pasta sauce, rosemary and garlic if using.
5. Cover. Simmer for 30 minutes.

Rice

1. Heat the oil in a saucepan. Add the onion and cook over a low heat for 5-8 minutes until soft. Add the rice and toss to coat in the oil until it whitens.
2. Add the hot water or stock and salt. Stir, cover and simmer gently for 12 minutes until tender. Stand for 5 minutes before fluffing with a fork.

Meatballs
in Madras
Curry

This recipe can also be made with Wattie's Indian Tomatoes in place of the Madras Curry Sauce. For a variation, make the meatballs with lean pork mince.

INGREDIENTS

- ½ cup red lentils
- 1 onion, peeled and finely diced
- 500 grams **Quality Mark Lean Minced Beef**
- 1 egg
- 1 tsp each ground coriander, cumin and garam masala, or use 1 tblsp curry powder
- 1 tsp salt
- 1 tsp black pepper
- 2 tblsp oil
- 415 gram can **Wattie's Madras Curry Sauce**
- 3 large tomatoes, finely chopped
- ¼ cup chopped fresh coriander or parsley

Garnish
- Plain unsweetened yoghurt and fresh coriander leaves

METHOD

1. Soak the lentils in 1 cup water for 30 minutes. Drain well.

2. In a bowl mix together the lentils, onion, mince, egg, coriander, cumin, garam masala or curry powder, salt and pepper. Shape into 12 even-sized meatballs.

3. Heat the oil in a lidded frying pan and brown the meatballs on all sides over a moderate heat.

4. Add the curry sauce and tomatoes and stir. Cover and simmer gently for 30 minutes until the meatballs are cooked. Stir in the chopped coriander or parsley.

   Serve over boiled rice garnished with yoghurt and coriander.

Cook's Tip

Red lentils can be found in the bulk bin section of the supermarket. If you cannot find them, use long-grain rice; but do not use brown lentils here.

Preparation Time 40 minutes

Cooking Time 40 minutes

Serves 4

Pork *with* Courgettes

Chinese five-spice powder is sweet, fragrant and slightly pungent. It contains star anise, cloves, fennel seed, cinnamon and Szechuan peppercorns. It can be found in the spice section of the supermarket or in Asian food shops. Keep it on hand to add 'oompf' to your Asian dishes.

INGREDIENTS

- grated rind and juice of one orange
- ¼ cup honey
- 2 tsp Chinese five-spice powder
- 1 kg thick-sliced pork slices
- dash of oil
- 4 courgettes, trimmed and sliced
- 425 gram can **Wattie's Sweet Chilli Stir-fry Sauce**
- ¼ cup **Wattie's Tomato Sauce**

Garnish (optional)
- 150 grams cooked prawns
- a few toasted cashew nuts

METHOD

1. Mix the orange rind and juice with the honey and five-spice powder. Toss the pork in this mixture and leave to marinate for up to 8 hours: the longer the better.

2. Grill the pork slices under a high heat for 10 minutes each side or until well cooked and crispy. Cut into 1-cm-wide slices.

3. Heat the oil in a frying pan and quickly cook the courgettes over a moderately high heat until browned, but do not over-cook. Add the stir-fry sauce, tomato sauce and pork and toss to heat all ingredients through.

Serve garnished with the prawns and cashew nuts if wished.

Preparation Time 10 minutes

Marinating Time 30 minutes-8 hours

Cooking Time 25-30 minutes

Serves 4

Cook's Tip

When marinating meat, rather than putting it in a container use a snap-lock bag; this makes it easier to cover the meat with the marinade and it can be easily turned over.

Chicken
with Gourmet BBQ Sauce *and* Drunken Fruit

INGREDIENTS

- ▶ ½ cup sherry
- ▶ ¼ cup sultanas
- ▶ ¼ cup dried apricots
- ▶ 4 Tegel Tender Basted Chicken Leg and Thigh Portions
- ▶ ½ bottle **Wattie's Bit on the Side Gourmet BBQ Sauce**

Garnish
- ▶ 1 orange, peeled and segmented
- ▶ 2 spring onions, trimmed and finely chopped, or 2 tblsp chopped thyme

METHOD

1. Heat the sherry, sultanas and apricots in the microwave for 1 minute on high power (100%). Spread over the base of a 2-litre-capacity ovenproof dish.

2. Arrange the chicken leg and thigh portions on top.

3. Pour over the barbecue sauce. Cover with foil and cook for 20 minutes at 200°C. Remove the foil and cook for a further 40 minutes or until the chicken portions are well cooked. If the chicken begins to brown too much, cover with foil.

4. Garnish with the orange segments and spring onions (see Cook's Tip).

Preparation Time 5 minutes

Cooking Time 1 hour

Serves 4

In 1998 Tegel launched its new tender basted chicken portions on *Food in a Minute*. They were an instant success.

Cook's Tip

Recipes sometimes call for a 'segmented orange'; this is very easy to do and looks much nicer than chopped orange with pieces of pith left on. Take an orange and cut off a thick slice of peel from the top and bottom so you have no white pith. With a sharp paring knife carefully take thick slices from the top to the bottom, following the curve of the orange. Continue right around the orange

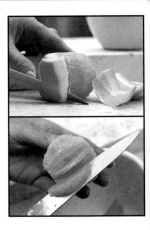

until all the peel and white pith is removed. Hold the orange in your hand with a small bowl underneath to catch the juice. Cut down on either side of each segment, leaving the membrane behind.

Chicken Pot *in a*

With everything cooked in the same pot, this meal can be served just as it is, or with a green vegetable on the side.

- 4 tblsp oil
- 1 onion, peeled and chopped
- 2 stalks celery, trimmed and chopped
- 500 gram bag **Wattie's Frozen Baby Carrots**
- 6-8 pieces **Tegel Boneless Chicken Thighs**
- 550 gram can **Wattie's Just Add Spicy Tomato and Chicken Simmer Sauce**
- 2 potatoes, well scrubbed, not peeled

METHOD

1. Heat half the oil in a large frying pan and quickly brown the onion and celery. Transfer to a large, 3-litre-capacity casserole.

2. Sprinkle the frozen carrots over the vegetables.

3. Return the pan to the heat and add the remaining oil. Quickly brown the chicken thighs over a high heat.

4. Arrange the chicken thighs on top of the vegetables. Pour the simmer sauce evenly over the top.

5. Cut the potatoes into thin slices and overlap evenly over the top.

6. Cover and cook at 180°C for 1¼ hours until the potatoes are tender and the chicken cooked.

Preparation Time 10 minutes

Cooking Time 1½ hours

Serves 4-6

Alan Gillard has continued over the last two years to take all the beautiful photographs of our *Food in a Minute* food shots. In addition he travelled with us to Spain to see the harvest of the elusive spice saffron. I caught him at work with my own camera.

Nasi Goreng

This basic recipe was a real favourite with viewers, and if you feel like jazzing it up even more see the variations listed below.

Variations

- Add finely shredded cooked chicken with the vegetables.
- Add finely chopped bacon with the onions and garlic.
- Cook the rice with 1-2 tsp ground turmeric so you have a wonderful golden Nasi Goreng.
- Add toasted cashew nuts with the rice.
- Sprinkle in a little Chinese five-spice powder with the paprika and salt.
- Flake smoked fish and toss through with the rice.
- Beat 2-3 eggs together and cook into an omelette; cool, slice finely and toss through the rice.
- For a new look and taste, use speciality mushrooms like shiitake or oyster mushrooms.

Preparation Time 15 minutes

Cooking Time 10 minutes

Serves 4

INGREDIENTS

- 2 tblsp oil
- 2 onions, peeled and finely sliced
- 2 cloves garlic, crushed, peeled and finely sliced
- 300 grams mushrooms, finely sliced
- 3 cups **Wattie's Frozen Cantonese Vegetables**
- 3 cups cooked long-grain rice, chilled
- 2 tblsp soy sauce
- 2 tblsp **Wattie's Tomato Sauce**
- 1 tsp each paprika and salt
- dash of chilli powder

METHOD

1. Heat the oil in a large frying pan or wok. Add the onion and cook over a high heat for about 2 minutes.

2. Add the garlic and mushrooms and continue to cook for a further minute. Add the frozen vegetables and toss over a high heat.

3. Once the vegetables are nearly warmed through, add the cooked, cold, long-grain rice and toss quickly to heat.

4. Mix together the soy sauce, tomato sauce, paprika, salt and chilli powder and toss into the rice. Serve piled high in a dish with sliced cucumber, diced tomatoes and crispy fried onions.

Crispy Fried Onions

To make crispy fried onions, cook 2 finely sliced onions in 2-3 tablespoons of oil in a hot pan until the onion has become quite brown and crispy. Drain well on absorbent paper before using.

Roasted Turkey *with Mango and Orange* Salsa

INGREDIENTS

- 1 frozen **Tegel Turkey Boneless Roll**, defrosted
- 10 rashers rindless streaky bacon

Mango and Orange Salsa
- 400 gram can **Wattie's Mangoes in Light Syrup**, well drained
- 2 oranges
- 3-4 spring onions, trimmed and finely chopped
- 2 tsp finely minced fresh ginger
- 2 tblsp honey
- 1 tblsp chopped fresh parsley
- 1 tblsp chopped fresh mint
- salt and pepper to season

METHOD

1. Carefully snip the netting off the turkey roll, leaving the thin skin underneath intact.

2. Wrap the streaky bacon rashers around the turkey roll so that they overlap, and secure with toothpicks.

3. Place on a rack over a baking dish and cook at 180°C for 1½ hours. Stand for 5 minutes before removing the toothpicks. Serve sliced either hot or cold with Mango and Orange Salsa.

Mango and Orange Salsa

1. Cut the mangoes into small dice.

2. Grate the rind from the orange, then peel away and discard the thick, white, bitter pith. Segment the flesh finely.

3. In a bowl blend together the mangoes, orange rind and flesh, spring onions, ginger, honey, parsley and mint. Season with salt and pepper.

Makes 2 cups

It's always a challenge looking for a new way to prepare turkey for Christmas on *Food in a Minute*, especially when we only have one minute to show you how to cook it. Last year I jazzed up a Tegel Boneless Turkey Roll with bacon and served it with a fresh fruit salsa. Delicious hot or cold, this proved very popular with viewers.

Defrosting Time 24 hours

Preparation Time 20 minutes

Cooking Time 1½ hours

Serves 6-8

Barbecue Tomato
Chicken
with
Cucumber
and Peach Relish

INGREDIENTS

▶ 8 pieces **Tegel Barbecue Tomato Chicken Pieces**, defrosted

Cucumber and Peach Relish
▶ 2 peaches, finely chopped
▶ ½ cucumber, finely chopped
▶ 2 stalks celery, finely chopped
▶ ½ cup natural unsweetened yoghurt
▶ 1 tblsp chopped fresh coriander
▶ 1 tblsp chopped fresh mint
▶ pepper to season

METHOD

1 Cook the defrosted chicken pieces on the barbecue over a moderately low heat for 45-50 minutes, turning regularly until cooked thoroughly.

Serve the chicken with the Cucumber and Peach Relish.

Cucumber and Peach Relish

1 In a bowl toss together the chopped peaches, cucumber, celery, yoghurt, coriander, mint and pepper and refrigerate for up to 2 hours before using.

Defrosting Time) Allow overnight

Cooking Time) 50 minutes

Serves) 4

Cook's Tip

If you find that the Tegel Barbecue Tomato Chicken is browning too quickly, lower the heat.

Fruit relish makes a refreshing accompaniment to barbecue food. This recipe appeared late in 1998 and uses fresh peaches, but you could easily substitute apricots or nectarines.

Christmas was a time for the crew to get together for a family barbecue. Director Rob McLaughlin made his home available and we all took a plate. Somehow Sarah-Jane still managed to find herself behind the barbecue giving Rob a hand with the cooking!

Thai Scented Burgers

The flavours of Thai food are some of my favourites: mint, lemon grass, ginger, garlic, coriander, kaffir lime leaves and chilli all add excitement to food.

INGREDIENTS

- ▶ 500 grams **Quality Mark Lean Minced Beef**
- ▶ 2-3 tender lemon tree leaves, finely sliced, or 2 tblsp chopped lemon grass
- ▶ 1 tblsp grated fresh ginger
- ▶ 3 cloves garlic, crushed, peeled and chopped
- ▶ 2 tsp ground coriander
- ▶ 1 tsp each salt and pepper
- ▶ 2 tblsp chopped fresh mint
- ▶ 2 tblsp chopped fresh coriander
- ▶ 2 spring onions, trimmed and chopped
- ▶ 1 cup fresh breadcrumbs
- ▶ 1 egg
- ▶ ½ cup **Wattie's Bit on the Side Sweet Chilli Sauce**

To Serve
- ▶ buns
- ▶ pineapple slices
- ▶ lettuce leaves

Cook's Tip

Lemon grass is literally a tall, reedy, lemon-scented grass. It grows well in the tropics, whereas lemons don't, hence its popularity in Asia, especially for Thai dishes. You can obtain it fresh or bottled: either way it's great to use. If you do not have any on hand, use lemon leaves as I have done.

Preparation Time 40 minutes

Cooking Time 15 minutes

Serves 4-6

METHOD

1. In a bowl put the mince, lemon leaves or lemon grass, ginger, garlic, ground coriander, salt and pepper, fresh mint and coriander, spring onions, breadcrumbs, egg and chilli sauce and mix well. If you can, allow the mixture to stand for about 30 minutes.

2. Mould into 6 even-shaped burgers.

3. Barbecue or pan-fry the burgers over a moderate heat for 5-7 minutes each side, turning only once. Alternatively, grill the burgers.

4. Serve the burgers on a grilled or toasted bun, with a slice of grilled pineapple and crispy lettuce.

INGREDIENTS

- ▶ 1 medium or large **Tegel Chicken**
- ▶ 1 orange, quartered
- ▶ 6 large garlic cloves
- ▶ 2 small branches of rosemary
- ▶ salt and pepper
- ▶ 820 gram can **Wattie's Whole Baby Beetroot**
- ▶ 2 tblsp honey

METHOD

1. Wash the chicken and pat dry inside and out. Push the orange quarters into the chicken cavity and hold the legs in place with a skewer.

2. Crush each garlic clove, but do not peel, and place in the base of a baking tray with the rosemary. Sit the chicken on top and season with salt and pepper.

3. Bake at 190°C for 1 hour.

4. Drain the beetroot and arrange these around the sides of the chicken. Continue cooking for a further 30 minutes until the chicken is tender. Turn the beetroot occasionally.

5. Transfer the chicken to a serving platter, cover and stand aside. Pour the honey on top of the beetroot and place over a moderate heat for about 1-2 minutes, shaking to coat the beetroot in the honey. Arrange on the platter with the chicken. Discard the rosemary branch before serving, but for garlic lovers, add the juicy roasted cloves to the serving platter.

   Serve with a salad.

Farmhouse Roast Chicken with Roasted Baby Beetroot

Baby beetroot makes a delicious roast vegetable and is well worth trying with your next roast chicken.

We celebrate the end of each session of *Food in a Minute* with an almond croissant morning tea. They've become a Friday special and here Sarah-Jane is in the middle of heating them up for the crew.

Preparation Time 10 minutes

Cooking Time 1½ hours

Serves 6

Curried Lamb
Pies with Ginger
Kumara
Mash

These are very delicious and ideal for a family meal or dinner party.

Cook's Tip

Naan bread is now available in the freezer section of your supermarket. This rustic Indian bread is made from a yeast and yoghurt dough, making it light and tasty. I like to spread naan bread with garlic butter, wrap it in foil and then reheat it in the oven. It's delicious this way. For a change, try butter flavoured with your favourite herbs or pastes.

Preparation Time 20 minutes

Cooking Time 20-25 minutes

Serves 4

INGREDIENTS

- 500 grams **Quality Mark Lean Leg Lamb Steaks**
- dash of oil
- ¼ cup **Wattie's Tomato Paste**
- 1 leek, trimmed, rinsed and finely chopped
- 1 carrot, peeled and finely chopped
- 415 gram can **Wattie's Rogan Josh Curry Sauce**

Ginger and Kumara Mash
- 750 grams kumara, peeled and chopped
- butter and milk for mashing
- 1 tsp ground ginger
- salt and pepper to season

METHOD

1 Cut the lamb steaks into 1 cm dice. Heat the oil in a frying pan and brown the meat over a high heat. Add the tomato paste and cook for 2-3 minutes, stirring until the paste becomes much darker in colour.

2 Stir in the leek, carrot and curry sauce. Lower the heat, cover and simmer for 10 minutes.

3 Divide the curry among four individual serving dishes and pile the ginger and kumara mash on top.

4 Bake at 200°C for 10 minutes.

Ginger and Kumara Mash

1 Cook the kumara in boiling salted water until tender. Drain and mash with a knob of butter and a good pour of milk. Add the ground ginger, season with salt and pepper and beat until smooth.

Beef
and Bean
Casserole

Hearty and ideal for winter, this is a basic casserole for a family meal.

INGREDIENTS

▸ 500 grams **Quality Mark Lean Chuck Steak**
▸ dash of oil
▸ 2 onions, peeled and cut into 2 cm dice
▸ 1 tblsp paprika
▸ 400 gram can **Wattie's Whole Peeled Tomatoes in Purée**
▸ 425 gram can **Craig's Mexican Beans**
▸ about 12 mushrooms, diced
▸ ½ cup beef stock or water

METHOD

1 Cut the chuck steak into large, 3 cm pieces.

2 Heat the oil in a frying pan and brown the meat over a moderate to high heat, then transfer to a casserole. This is best done in two batches.

3 Add the onion to the pan and cook for 2-3 minutes. Sprinkle over the paprika and cook for ½ minute before stirring in the tomatoes, beans, mushrooms and beef stock or water.

4 Bring the mixture to the boil and then pour over the beef. Cover and cook at 160°C for 1¼ hours until the meat is tender.

Serve hot with your favourite green vegetable.

Cook's Tip

If you are cooking for one or two, freeze half the casserole for another day. Allow it to cool completely and pack in airtight containers, leaving enough room for expansion as it freezes. Defrost in the refrigerator before thoroughly reheating.

Preparation Time 20 minutes
Cooking Time 1½ hours
Serves 4

INGREDIENTS

- 25 grams butter
- 1 onion, peeled and finely chopped
- 2 tsp minced garlic
- 2 cups short-grain rice
- 1 cup dry white wine
- 3½ cups chicken stock
- 425 gram can **Wattie's Condensed Mushroom Soup**
- ½ cup grated parmesan cheese
- ¼ cup cream
- salt and pepper to season

To Serve
- mushrooms, bacon rashers, parsley

METHOD

1. Heat the butter in a large saucepan, add the onion and cook over a moderately low heat for 5-8 minutes until very soft but not coloured. Add the garlic and cook a further minute.

2. Add the rice and stir in the butter and onion mixture until the rice begins to change to a white colour.

3. Add the wine and stir constantly over a moderately low heat until the rice has absorbed all the wine.

4. Add the chicken stock to the risotto, ½ cup at a time, stirring continuously. When each amount has been absorbed add the next measure.

5. When all the stock has been added, stir in the mushroom soup and continue to stir over a low heat until the risotto is thick and creamy.

6. Stir in the parmesan cheese and cream and season with salt and pepper. Serve over grilled mushrooms and crispy bacon rashers with chopped parsley to garnish.

Creamy Mushroom Risotto

Risottos are very filling and truly delicious. They take a little time to make, but the more you stir it the creamier the risotto will be.

Cook's Tip

Parmesan cheese from Italy is a taste sensation. If you have sworn off parmesan after eating the dried version found in shaker packs, think again and give it a try. I like it best in thin slices with fresh pears, or tossed in a salad or used to garnish a risotto.

Preparation Time 15 minutes

Cooking Time 30-40 minutes

Serves 4-6

Fish
in Sweet
Curry Sauce

Wattie's Indian Spiced Tomatoes are my favourite product in its tomato range. They have plenty of flavour, ideal for making instant curry dishes like this one.

Nick Tresidder has continued to work with us over the last two years, photographing many of the *Food in a Minute* recipes. If we receive the thumbs up from Nick's four young boys we are pretty sure the recipe will be a great hit with viewers. Here we captured Nick working on the front cover shoot.

INGREDIENTS

- 2 x 400 gram cans **Wattie's Indian Spiced Tomatoes**
- 4 x 150 gram pieces firm white fish fillets (hapuka is great)
- 1–1½ cups **Wattie's Frozen Cross Cut Green Beans**
- 2 tblsp chopped fresh coriander

Banana and Ginger Raita
- 1 banana, peeled and diced
- 1 cup non-fat unsweetened yoghurt
- 1 tsp minced fresh ginger
- pinch of salt

METHOD

1. Put the tomatoes into a lidded frying pan and simmer gently until they are reduced by one third.

2. Arrange the fish fillets on top in one layer and cook for 3 minutes.

3. Turn the fish over and sprinkle the green beans on top.

4. Cover and simmer gently for 5-8 minutes until the fish is cooked. Sprinkle over the chopped coriander. The cooking time will depend on the thickness of the fish fillets.

Serve on rice with the Banana and Ginger Raita and poppadums.

Banana and Ginger Raita

Mix all ingredients together.

Preparation Time 10 minutes

Cooking Time 20-25 minutes

Serves 4

Sausage Hot Pot

Sausage meat can be quickly turned into a delicious and economical meal, and it also makes a change from traditional sausages.

Preparation Time 10 minutes

Cooking Time 30-40 minutes

Serves 4

INGREDIENTS

- 500 grams sausage meat
- ¼ cup chopped parsley
- ¼ cup **Wattie's Tomato Sauce**
- pepper to season
- 1 apple, peeled and grated
- 1 egg
- dash of oil
- 560 gram can **Wattie's Just Add Brown Onion Simmer Sauce**

METHOD

1. In a bowl mix together the sausage meat, parsley, tomato sauce, pepper, apple and egg.

2. Using wet hands, roll the mixture into 20 even-shaped balls.

3. Heat the oil in a lidded frying pan and brown the sausage balls evenly on all sides.

4. Add the brown onion sauce, stir, cover and simmer for 30 minutes over a low heat.

Serve with your favourite vegetables.

Port grapes are harvested from the vines that seem to struggle to grow on the steep, terraced hills in the Douro Valley of Portugal. The history of port grapes is as fascinating as the magnificent country where they are harvested. Our view here is over Pinhao in the Douro Valley. Each company has its own workforce and at the time of our visit, autumn, the men were pruning the vines. Lunch is prepared by a cook and served to the workers out in the fields. I was fortunate enough to oversee the lunch for Graham's workers. It consisted mainly of salted cod – a traditional Portuguese dish.

Chickpea *and* Pumpkin *Casserole*

A delicious alternative to a meat casserole. I like to add a few olives just before serving – and chopped coriander.

During our visit to La Mancha, central Spain, we were hosted by Mr Valerino Gonzalez at an annual family harvest of saffron in the tiny village of San Pedro. I joined a group of local women huddled around the table in a country farmhouse who explained (by sign language as I spoke no Spanish and they no English) how to pluck the precious stamin from the crocus flower. Sustenance was a piece of ham, home cured and carved off the bone to eat as they worked. Home-cured hams hung from the rafters, and peppers, hanging to dry in the last of the late summer's sun, lined the curtain rails. Saffron is worth NZ$2000 per kilogram, so it's a particularly important cash crop for these country folk.

INGREDIENTS

- dash of oil
- 1 onion, peeled and finely chopped
- 1 tblsp minced garlic
- 1 tblsp paprika
- 500–600 grams pumpkin, peeled
- 300 gram can **Craig's Chickpeas**, well drained
- 400 gram can **Wattie's Tomatoes and Courgettes**
- ½ cup raisins
- 1 cup vegetable stock or water
- 12 Brussels sprouts, trimmed and halved, or 2 cups broccoli florets
- salt and pepper to taste

METHOD

1. Heat the oil in a flame-proof casserole or lidded frying pan. Add the onion and cook for 3-5 minutes until soft.

2. Add the garlic and paprika and cook for a further minute.

3. Cut the pumpkin into 2 cm pieces and add to the pan with the chickpeas, tomatoes and courgettes, raisins and stock or water. Cover and simmer for 10 minutes.

4. Add the Brussels sprouts or broccoli to the casserole, cover and simmer for a further 5 minutes or until the vegetables are tender. Season with salt and pepper before serving over rice.

Preparation Time 15 minutes

Cooking Time 20-25 minutes

Serves 4

INGREDIENTS

- 2 x **Quality Mark Loins of Lamb**, (each with 6-7 chops)
- **Lea and Perrins Worcestershire Sauce**
- 1 tsp minced garlic
- pepper
- 2 onions, peeled and sliced
- 2 parsnips, peeled and sliced thickly
- 250 grams pumpkin, sliced (see Cook's Tip)
- dash of oil
- ½ 500 gram packet **Wattie's Frozen Whole Baby Beans**
- ½ cup **ETA Garden Herb or French Dressing**

METHOD

1. Score the lamb loins on the skin side and season well with Worcestershire sauce. Turn and season the meat well with the sauce, garlic and pepper. Tie the flap securely with string.

2. Toss the onions, parsnips and pumpkin in the dash of oil and place in a shallow roasting dish. Sit the lamb loins on top.

3. Fan bake at 200°C for 35 minutes.

4. Transfer the lamb to a plate and sprinkle the baby beans into the baking dish, toss and return to the oven for 5 minutes. Remove and toss the vegetables with the dressing.

5. Carve the lamb into chops and serve over the hot vegetable salad.

Quick Roast Lamb

My brother Adrian loves cooking and a roasted loin of lamb is high on his list of favourites. It's economical, quick and very tasty and here I served it with a hot roast vegetable salad.

Cook's Tip

I prefer to use the top half of a butternut pumpkin for this recipe, cut into 1-cm-wide rings and then halved to make semi-circles.

Preparation Time 20 minutes

Cooking Time 40 minutes

Serves 4-6

desserts
and baking

Tempting puddings, steaming hot muffins or chilled icecream sweet treats are always enjoyable. This chapter is probably my favourite as I am a true dessert lover. In here you'll find the old-fashioned self-saucing pudding made easy, muffins loaded with tropical flavours, the delicious Chocolate Mayonnaise cake and a twist on the traditional Christmas Pud. This is a chapter to indulge in and enjoy.

Easy Summer Christmas Pudding

If you're looking for a new family Christmas pudding – try this one. A delicate fruit sponge steamed over golden plums makes a delicious twist on an old favourite.

Cake Variation

Grease a 24 cm spring-form cake tin with the 1 tablespoon of butter. Sprinkle with the sugar and arrange the plums and walnuts over the base and spread the cake mixture on top. Bake at 180°C for 60 minutes.

Cook's Tip

Walnuts and other nuts including coconut will go rancid quickly if left in a warm kitchen cupboard. Keep them in the freezer and lightly toast them in a 180°C oven for 10–12 minutes to bring them to life.

INGREDIENTS

- 820 gram can **Wattie's Golden Plums in Syrup**, well drained
- 1 tblsp butter for greasing
- 2 tblsp brown sugar
- about 8 walnut halves
- 410 gram can **Wattie's Fruit**; apricots, nectarines or peaches, well drained
- 75 grams butter, softened
- ¾ cup caster sugar
- grated rind of two large oranges
- 2 eggs
- 1¾ cups self-raising flour
- ½ cup milk

METHOD

1. Halve the plums and remove the stone.
2. Butter a 2.5 litre pudding basin with the 1 tablespoon of butter and sprinkle over the brown sugar.
3. Place a walnut half in the centre of half the plums and place these cut side down in the base of the pudding bowl.
4. Finely chop the remaining plums and the canned fruit.
5. Beat the butter, sugar and orange rind together until thick and creamy. Beat in the eggs one at a time.
6. Fold in the sifted flour and diced fruits alternately with the milk. Pile the cake mixture into the pudding bowl over the plums.
7. Cover with 2 layers of greaseproof paper and 1 of foil. Secure with string. Steam on a trivet in a saucepan of boiling water for 1¾ hours.

Preparation Time 15 minutes

Cooking Time 1¾ hours for pudding, 60 minutes for cake

Serves 8-10

Creamy *Tropical* Muffins

This muffin recipe needs the zest of a couple of oranges or lemons to enhance the tropical fruit.

Cook's Tip

Grease your muffin tins even if they're non-stick as this will help your tins last longer.

If you do not have any **Wattie's Tropical Fruit Salad Chunks**, use any other **Wattie's** fruit, making sure it's the same can size.

Adding the rind of a grated lemon is a quick way to add plenty of flavour to an endless number of dishes. When my Mum grated the rind of a lemon, Dad used the juice to clean his hands and smooth off any roughness. Squeeze the juice into the palm of one hand and add a tablespoon or two of sugar. Rub your hands together well and then rinse thoroughly. Apply handcream afterwards and you'll find you have beautifully smooth hands.

INGREDIENTS

▶ 2 cups flour
▶ 1 tsp baking soda
▶ 2 tsp baking powder
▶ ½ cup sugar
▶ 1 cup bran
▶ 425 gram can **Wattie's Tropical Fruit Salad Chunks**
▶ 1 egg
▶ ¾ cup fruit salad yoghurt
▶ grated rind 2 oranges or lemons
▶ 100 grams butter, melted
▶ about ½ cup cream cheese

METHOD

1 Sift the flour, baking soda, baking powder and sugar into a bowl. Stir in the bran.

2 Put the fruit chunks with the juice, egg, fruit salad yoghurt and orange rind into a food processor and process until evenly and finely chopped.

3 Pour the fruit into the dry ingredients and fold together, adding in the butter as you go.

4 Half-fill 12 well greased muffin tins. Place a teaspoon of cream cheese in the centre of each and top with the remaining muffin mixture.

5 Bake at 220°C for 15-18 minutes until well risen and golden. Cool in the tin for 5 minutes before serving.

Preparation Time 15 minutes
Cooking Time 20 minutes
Makes 12

Apple *and* Date Loaf

INGREDIENTS

- 1 cup chopped dried dates
- 1 tsp baking soda
- 400 gram can **Wattie's Simply Apple**
- 2 tblsp finely chopped crystallised ginger
- 2 tsp ground ginger
- ¼ cup boiling water
- 2 tblsp softened butter
- ¾ cup sugar
- 1 egg
- 2 cups self-raising flour, sifted

METHOD

1. In a bowl put the dates, baking soda, apple, crystallised ginger, ground ginger and boiling water and stir well.

2. In another bowl mix the butter and sugar together and then beat in the egg. Gradually stir in the date mixture and sifted flour.

3. Spoon into a greased, floured and bottom-lined 25 cm x 11 cm x 7 cm loaf tin.

4. Bake at 180°C for 1 hour or until the loaf is cooked when tested with a skewer.

   Cool in the tin for 10 minutes before turning out onto a cake rack to cool. Serve sliced with butter or a slice of cheddar cheese for a change.

Preparation Time 15 minutes

Cooking Time 1 hour

Makes 1

One of my first cooking experiences was baking a date loaf. There was always one in the cake tin; dates were easy to obtain and loaves kept well. This one is exceptionally moist and tastes better if it's a day or two old before cutting a slice. In our house the slices would be liberally spread with butter.

Cook's Tip

- Use New Zealand dried apricots in place of dates.
- Use mixed peel in place of crystallised ginger and replace the ground ginger with mixed spice or ground cardamom.
- Use brown sugar in place of white sugar.

INGREDIENTS

- 2 cups self-raising flour
- ¼ cup sugar
- 100 grams butter
- 1 egg
- 1 cup milk
- 1 tsp vanilla essence

Sauce
- 375 gram jar **Craig's Black Doris Plum Jam**
- 1 cup boiling water

METHOD

1 Sift the flour and sugar into a bowl.

2 Rub in the butter until the mixture forms coarse crumbs.

3 Blend the egg, milk and vanilla essence together and pour into the dry ingredients. Mix together gently.

4 Spread the batter over the base of a well-greased, 2-litre-capacity pie dish.

5 Mix the plum jam with the boiling water and pour carefully over the top of the batter.

6 Bake at 180°C for 35-45 minutes until the pudding is golden and well risen.

7 Stand for 5 minutes before serving, as the sauce is very hot. Serve hot with whipped cream.

Preparation Time 15 minutes

Cooking Time 45 minutes

Serves 6

Black Doris Plum
Self-saucing Pud

Old-fashioned desserts like those my mother made are still my favourites, especially in winter. Warwick and I never spare ourselves on the cream either; it's usually whipped and slightly sweetened.

Cook's Tip

When rubbing butter into dry ingredients, give the bowl a shake at the end. If any large pieces of butter still remain, they will rise to the top and you can quickly rub them in. I prefer to use pure vanilla essence, made from vanilla pods, as the flavour and taste are superior to the imitation vanilla essence made as a by-product of the timber industry. Use the pure vanilla if you can; initially you may find it expensive, but you will use less of it as the flavour is more intense.

Chocolate *Mayonnaise* Cake

Mayonnaise is made from eggs and oil with flavourings and it can make an excellent moist chocolate cake. Use Wattie's Classic Mayonnaise only for this recipe to ensure success. If your cake dips in the middle just a little, don't worry: it will be just fine.

Cook's Tip

Add ¼ cup finely chopped nuts. Add 1 tblsp coffee powder with the hot water for a mocha version.

Mike O'Sullivan's two young boys, Tom and Mitchell, are firm *Food in a Minute* favourites and they pop into the set regularly to say 'Hi' and taste the food.

INGREDIENTS

- ¼ cup cocoa
- 1 cup hot water
- 1 tblsp vanilla essence
- 2 cups flour
- 2 tsp baking soda
- 1 cup caster sugar
- ¾ cup **Wattie's Classic Mayonnaise**

METHOD

1. Mix the cocoa, hot water and vanilla essence together in a jug. Cool.

2. Sift the flour, baking soda and sugar in a bowl and make a well in the centre.

3. Combine the mayonnaise with the cocoa mixture and then pour into the well. Mix together gently with a holed spoon.

4. Pour into a well greased and lined 20 cm round cake tin.

5. Bake at 180°C for 35-40 minutes until the cake is cooked when tested. Cool in the tin for 10 minutes before turning out onto a cake rack.

When cold, ice with your favourite chocolate icing, or with our Rich Chocolate Glaze, or simply dust with icing sugar to serve.

Rich Chocolate Glaze

Melt 125 grams dark chocolate with ½ cup cream together in the microwave for 1 minute. Stir to combine, cool a little and then pour over the cake and smooth out.

Preparation Time 30 minutes

Cooking Time 40 minutes

Makes 1

Hazelnut
and Rum-soaked
Prune
Icecream

This recipe was prepared with Weight Watchers Icecream, but you can use normal vanilla and chocolate icecream if you wish.

During the year I was fortunate enough to have my Mum and Dad visit Auckland while we were filming. Now well into their eighties, they were both royally treated by the fabulous *Food in a Minute* crew who took time out for a team photo with them.

INGREDIENTS

- 20 pitted prunes
- ¼ cup dark rum
- 2 tblsp sugar
- ½ cup toasted hazelnuts
- 950 ml carton **Weight Watchers Chocolate Icecream**
- ½ x 950 ml carton **Weight Watchers Vanilla Icecream**

METHOD

1. Finely slice the prunes and place in a jug with the rum and sugar. Microwave for 1 minute on high power, stir and then stand until cold.

2. Finely chop the hazelnuts in a blender.

3. Place the chocolate icecream in the microwave on defrost for 2 minutes. Working quickly, push half the softened chocolate icecream into the base of a 20 cm x 10 cm loaf tin. Sprinkle over half the hazelnuts and then spread half the prunes on top.

4. Soften the vanilla icecream as above and press half the icecream on top of the chocolate and prune layer. Sprinkle over the rest of the hazelnuts and spread out the prunes as above.

5. Spread the remaining chocolate icecream on top of the vanilla, nut and prune layer. Re-freeze for at least 4 hours, and preferably overnight, before serving. Re-freeze the unused vanilla icecream.

Preparation Time 15-20 minutes

Freezing Time at least 4 hours

Serves 8

Country Pikelets

INGREDIENTS

- 50 grams butter
- 410 gram can **Wattie's Peach Slices in Clear Juice**
- ½ cup plain yoghurt
- 1 cup milk
- 1 egg
- grated rind of 1 orange or lemon
- 2 cups wholemeal self-raising flour
- ¼ cup caster sugar

METHOD

1. Melt the butter in a frying pan and cook until it becomes nut brown. Place the frying pan immediately on a damp cloth to arrest any further cooking and to cool.

2. Strain the peaches, reserving the juice. Finely dice the fruit and place in a jug with the juice, yoghurt, milk, egg and orange rind. Gently mix together with a fork.

3. Put the flour and sugar into a bowl and fold in the fruit mixture and nut-brown butter.

4. Heat a knob of butter in a frying pan and place large spoonfuls of the mixture in the pan. Allow the pikelets to cook until bubbles rise to the surface. Turn and cook for a further 2 minutes. Transfer to a cake rack to cool while cooking with the remaining mixture.

Serve hot with honey and yoghurt.

Preparation Time 15 minutes

Cooking Time about 5 minutes each, 20 minutes whole batch

Serves 4

This is perfect for a lazy weekend brunch. Add a crispy slice of bacon and a few extra peaches to serve.

After three and a half years Rob McLaughlin still keeps us on our toes as he directs *Food in a Minute*. Alan Gillard caught him on camera here in full flight, giving instructions for our next move.

Store-cupboard Basics

Have you ever had guests – or your teenagers' friends – descend upon you unexpectedly and you opened up the store cupboard to find Mrs Hubbard had got there before you?

With a bit of clever buying you can build up your pantry cupboard and have an eclectic mix of foods that will come to the rescue next time you need a helping hand.

Here's an overview of what to have on hand. Not all these items are necessary, but some might be favourites and will jazz up a pizza – like olives, which if it wasn't for Warwick would not grace my cupboards; but then I'm always grateful when I have to throw a platter of nibbles together as I can spice them up or serve them as they are.

Dry-cupboard/Store-cupboard

• **Dry Goods** Flours, sugars, custard powder, dried fruits and a bar of chocolate are essential. With them you can whip up a special treat in no time.

• **Oils** A bottle for pan-frying and in summer maybe a bottle of olive oil for salads. If you like serving Asian food, sesame oil drizzled over a stir-fry before serving adds panache.

• **Vinegar** I prefer wine vinegars as they are good for dressings and preserves.

• **Spices** Buy small quantities as they do go stale. I like to have cardamom or ginger (great with fruits), cumin and coriander (essential in Mexican food), garam masala and a good curry powder for jazzing up Indian curries; salt and pepper are mainstays, as are a spice or two for baking, like cinnamon or mixed spice. Check out different brands, as you will find that each proprietary brand has a different blend.

• **Herbs** Use fresh herbs whenever you can; they're available in supermarkets these days. Dried thyme and dill are good stand-bys, but use them sparingly as when dried they are two to three times more powerful. To re-vamp dried herbs, pour over a little warm water and strain before use.

• **Rices, Other Starches** We have such a great choice today, it is almost confusing. Try to keep a short-grain rice for desserts or a paella and a long-grain rice to accompany curries and stir-fries. Two delicious varieties of long-grain rice now readily available are jasmine, ideal for Asian dishes, and Basmati, which is perfect for accompanying a special curry. Couscous and lentils have become fashionable and they both make a great change. To see how easy it is to cook couscous, see page 40.

• **Pasta** Spaghetti is always a great stand-by, but add a couple of shapes such as those pictured. Macaroni or penne are good choices. Egg noodles will add authenticity to your Asian dishes and can be served boiled or fried.

• **Alcohol** The golden rule is: Cook with wine that you will be happy to drink. Any off-flavours will only be enhanced when the wine is heated.

• **Sauces** Worcestershire, soy, hoisin, Tabasco, plum and tomato are all good to have on hand. I also keep Ketjap Manis (Indonesian soy sauce) as it is sweeter and delicious poured over fried rice.

• **Condiments** Have one or two Thai curry pastes on hand, like those prepared by Asian Home Gourmet, or A Taste of Thai. They can quickly help you quickly whip up a Thai curry or soup. Although I like to have fresh garlic and ginger, it is a good idea to keep a bottle of prepared garlic, ginger or chilli: store them in the refrigerator once they are opened. Then there is an endless array of chutneys, relishes and pickles: a spoonful of chutney added to a casserole will add new flavours, or pickles on a platter make instant nibbles.

Bottled olives or canned anchovies will liven up any instant nibble platter, pizza or casserole.

As for jams, it's up to you, but if you keep one or two of your favourites you'll find they can do much more than just be a topping on toast – for example, they can fill a jam tart, or add interest to a steamed pudding.

• **Canned Goods** Where would we be without kidney beans, canned vegetables like corn or asparagus, canned fruit like pears or peaches, or canned tomatoes? Wattie's have a fabulous variety of canned sauces for fast, tasty food like curry sauces or simmer sauces. Make sure you always have some of your favourites tucked away. Pear halves, drained, can become an upside-down tart, Indian tomatoes reduced make a divine sauce with Butter Chicken and a grilled steak has an instant sauce with Canned Mushrooms in Green Peppercorn Sauce.

Refrigerator

The standard foods – butter, milk, cheese – can be augmented with sour cream, yoghurt, fresh or other cheeses and cream. The refrigerator is also the place to store opened condiments and fresh fruits and vegetables.

Freezer

I can't live without my freezer, but be careful that it doesn't become a forgotten hidey-hole where you find mysterious unlabelled and undated packages. I keep frozen pastries here to whip up tarts or pies, nuts so they do not go rancid, rashers of bacon – fabulous for lazy weekend breakfasts – and soups or stocks. Also meat and chicken (but never fish as it is always best to buy and use fresh fish) and a bag or two of vegetables and berryfruits are good standbys.

This may seem a lot – but it is not really. Don't rush out and buy everything at once, but gradually build upon your basics list to add variety. Remember that a discounted product is not a bargain unless you are going to eat it; and always check what's in the cupboard before buying as there is no point having two of something unless it is needed.

Dry Cupboard

Refrigerator   Freezer

Index